TABLE OF CONTENTS

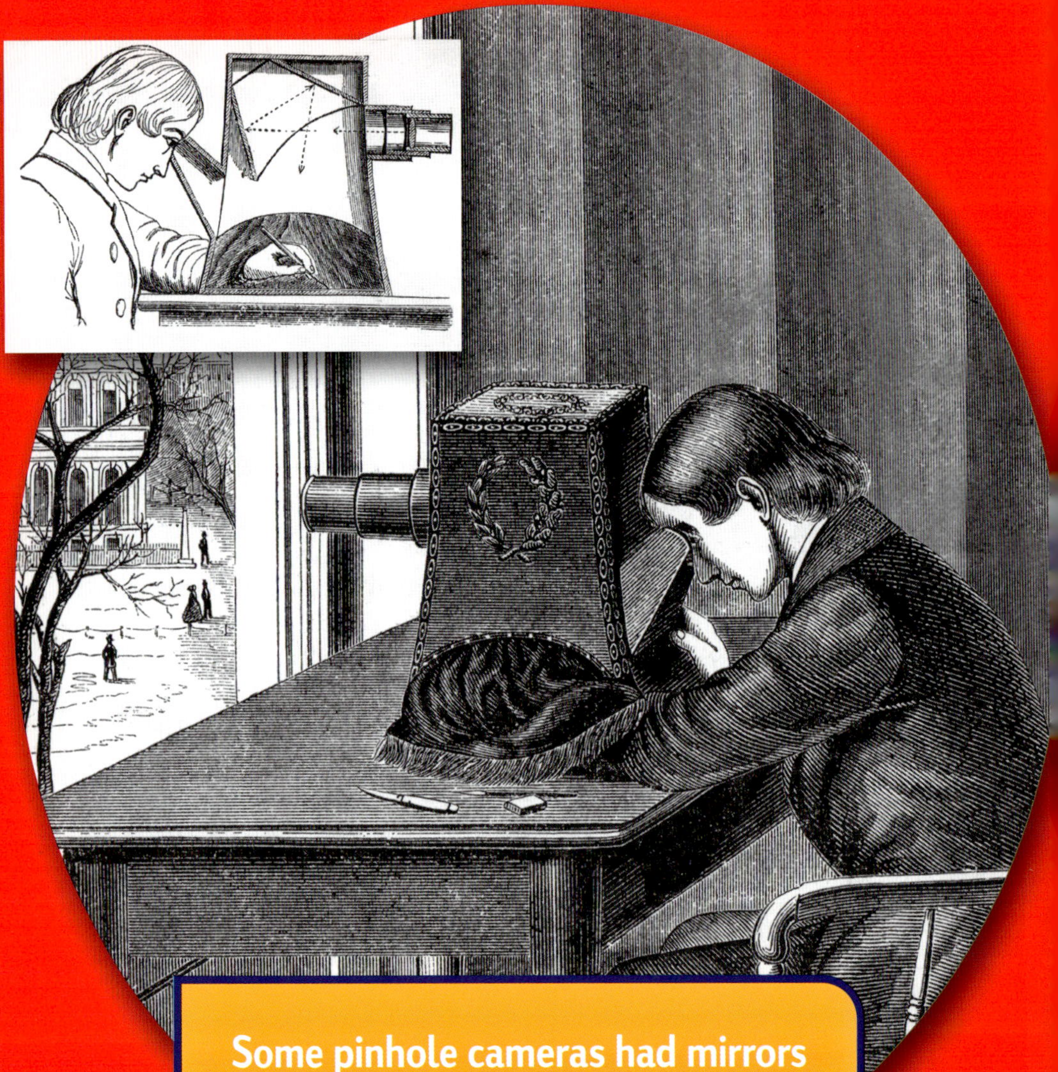

Some pinhole cameras had mirrors to direct light down so the artist could more easily trace the picture.

Artists use pinhole cameras to create pictures.

1500s

. . LOADING . . . LOADING .

The First Cameras

Pull out a cell phone. Snap a selfie! Taking pictures wasn't always so easy. Before cameras, the only pictures were drawings. In the 1500s, artists started using pinhole cameras to draw pictures. These boxes had a tiny hole to let in sunlight. A beam of light shined inside. It showed the view from outside. It made a "real" picture the artist could trace.

OADING . . . LOADING . . . LOADING . . .

Pinhole camera pictures could not make **prints**. Inventors looked for new ways to capture **images**. In 1827, Nicéphore Niépce found a way. He put a thin layer of black, sticky **bitumen** on a **plate**. Then he put the plate in his pinhole camera. The bitumen hardened where the light hit. After eight hours, a picture formed. It was the first photograph.

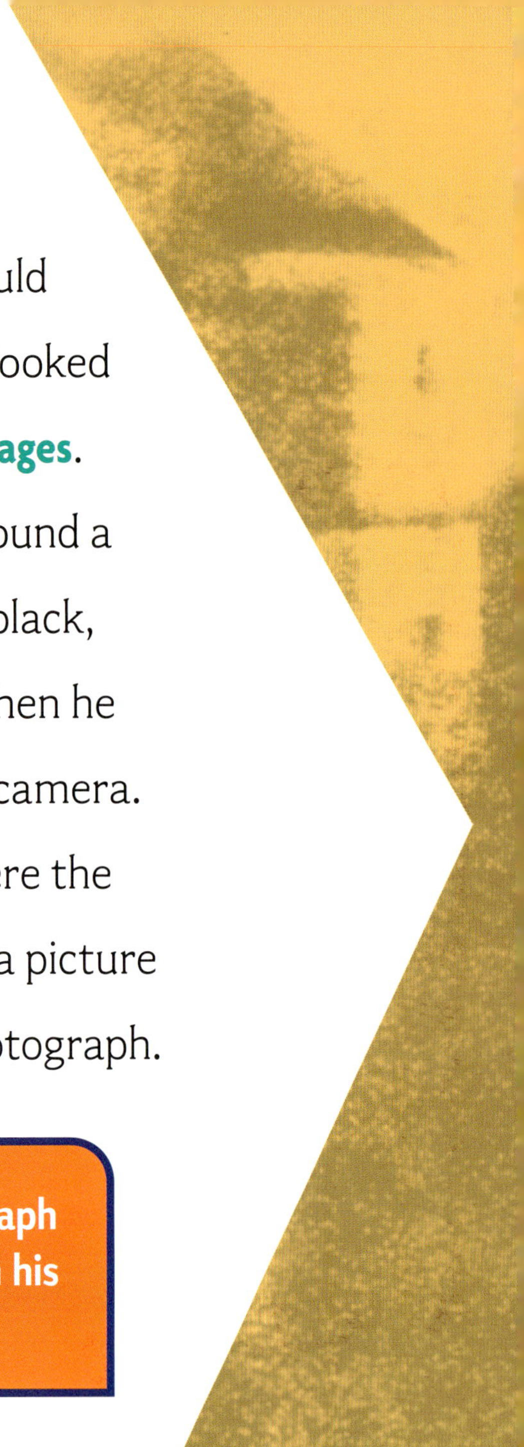

Niépce's (top) first photograph (inset) shows the view from his window in France.

Artists use pinhole cameras to create pictures.

1500s

1827

Nicéphore Niépce creates the first photograph.

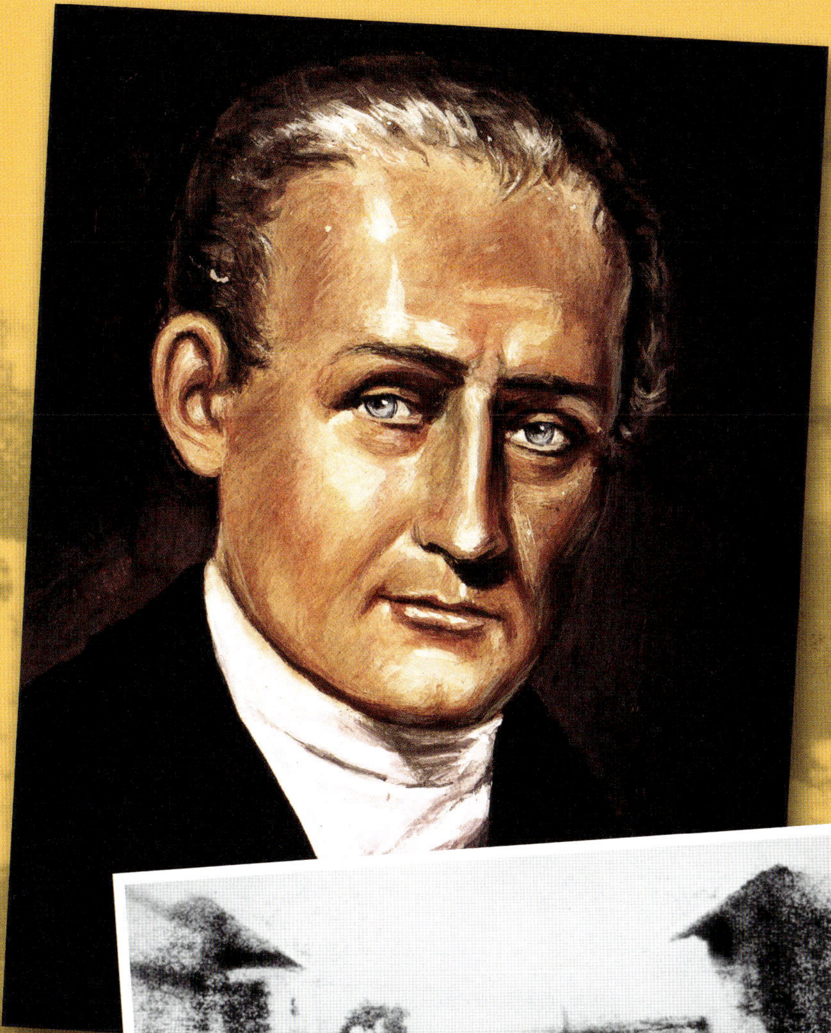

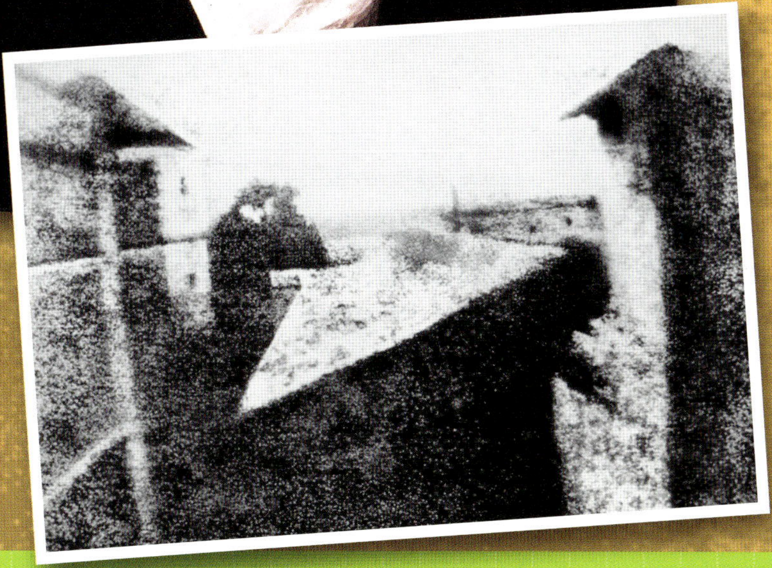

LOADING . . . LOADING . . . LOADING . . .

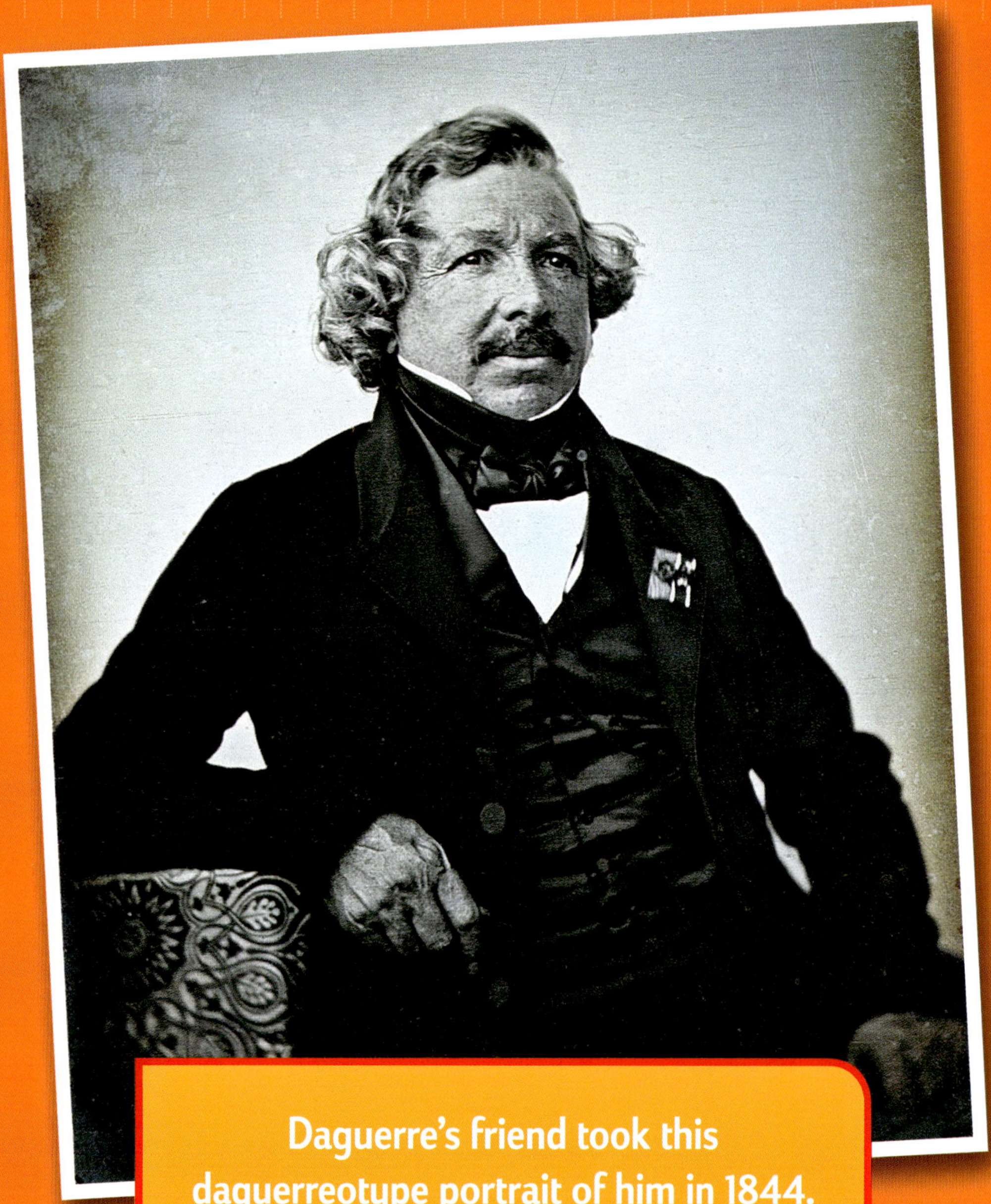

Daguerre's friend took this daguerreotype portrait of him in 1844.

1500s	1827	1839
Artists use pinhole cameras to create pictures.	Nicéphore Niépce creates the first photograph.	Louis Daguerre invents the daguerreotype camera.

G . . . LOADING .

Early Photography

No one wants to pose for eight hours. Niépce's partner, Louis Daguerre, worked to shorten that time. Daguerre used a plate coated with silver salts. The salts changed color in light. He then steamed the plates with mercury. The picture showed up faster. In 1839, he released the daguerreotype camera. It took pictures in just seconds.

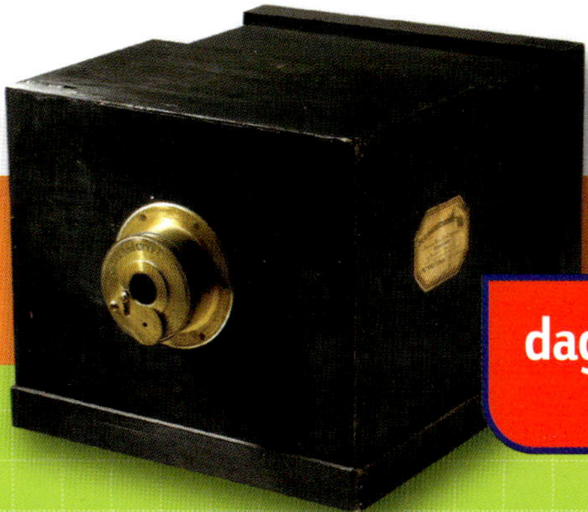

daguerreotype camera

LOADING... LOADING... LOADING...

Cameras use lenses to create pictures. Lenses bend light. Each lens shape changes the **focus** of the picture. The most popular pictures were people sitting or standing. In 1840, Charles Chevalier designed a lens for these portraits. Joseph Petzval soon designed a different portrait lens. Its focus helped pictures form faster. It became popular.

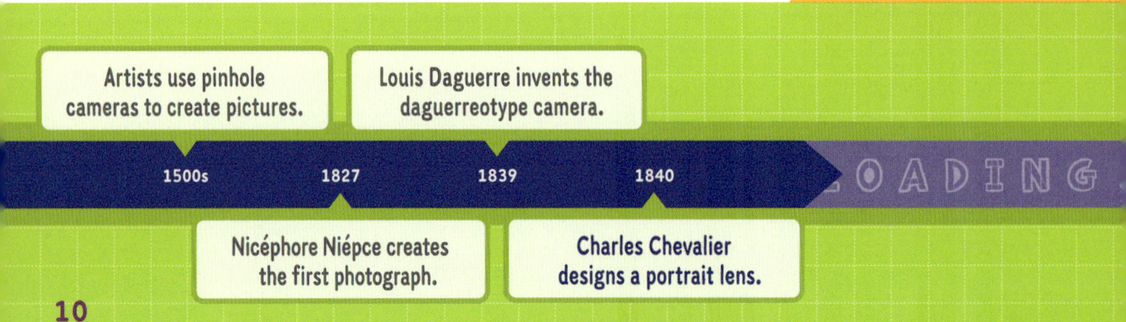

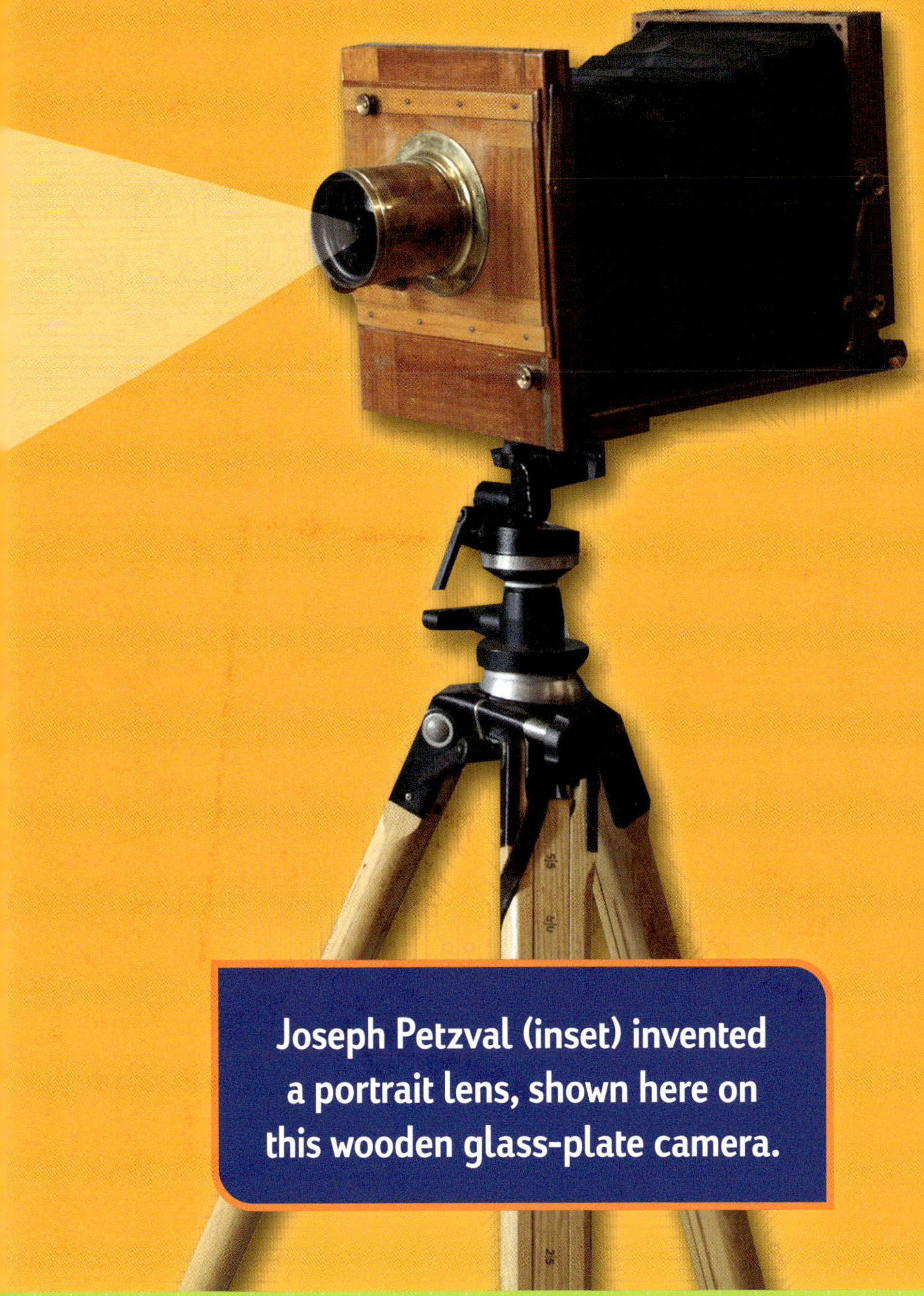

Joseph Petzval (inset) invented a portrait lens, shown here on this wooden glass-plate camera.

OADING . . . LOADING . . . LOADING . . .

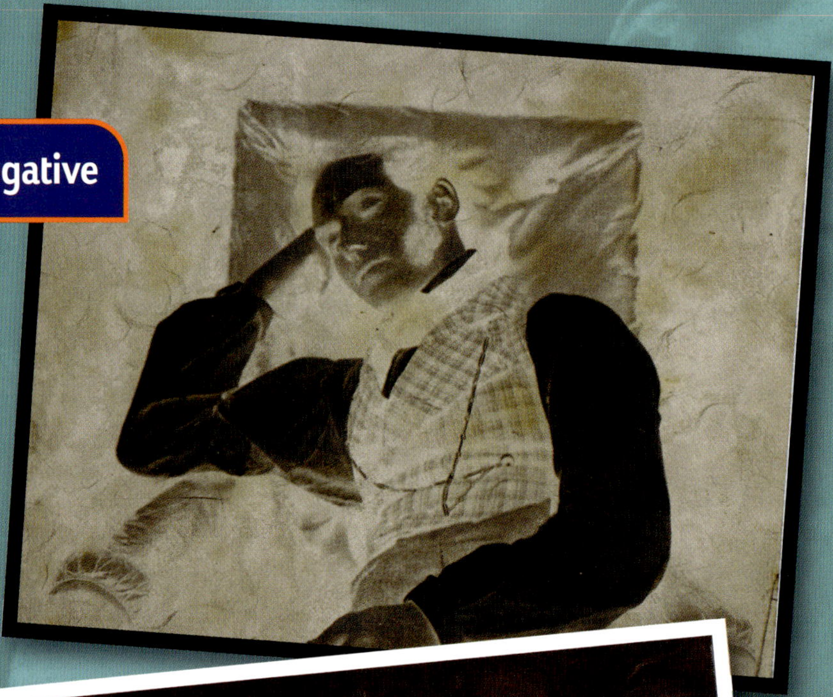

Negative

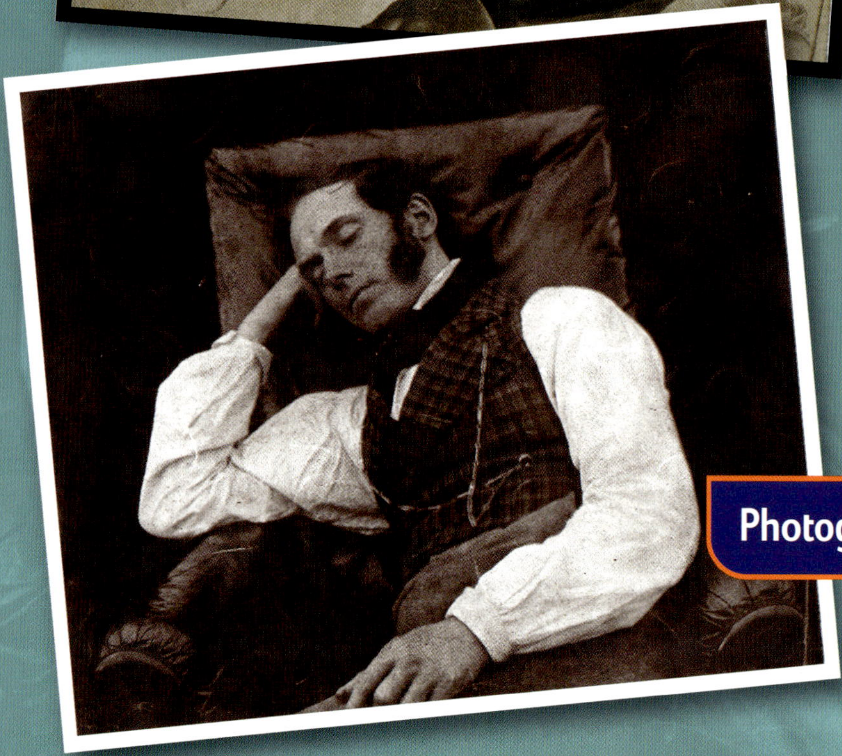

Photograph

Artists use pinhole cameras to create pictures.

Louis Daguerre invents the daguerreotype camera.

William Henry Fox Talbot discovers a way to make prints.

1500s | 1827 | 1839 | 1840 | 1841

Nicéphore Niépce creates the first photograph.

Charles Chevalier designs a portrait lens.

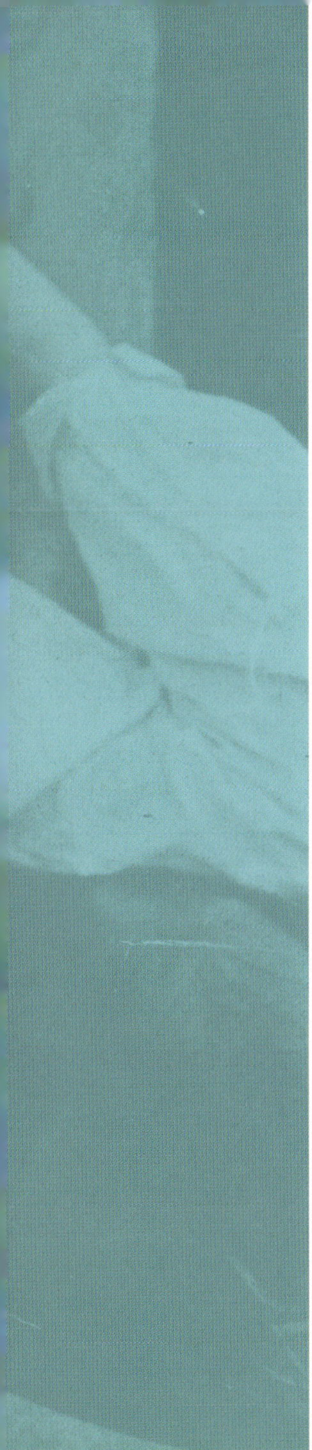

Daguerrerotype cameras created one picture. In 1841, William Henry Fox Talbot found a way to make more than one print. He used chemicals on paper. The image had the light and dark areas reversed. It was called a **negative**. He then used different chemicals to **develop** it. The light and dark switched back to make prints.

Talbot tested his process with subjects near him, including his assistant sleeping!

People tried different materials for negatives. In 1847, glass plates became popular. Glass made sharp pictures, but it was breakable. In 1889, Kodak invented a light, bendable **film** called **celluloid**. They put it in their first camera, the Kodak. People didn't worry about breaking glass. Anyone could take pictures anywhere. Snapshots became popular.

These snapshots were taken with the Kodak camera, which took round pictures on film.

- **1500s** — Artists use pinhole cameras to create pictures.
- **1827** — Nicéphore Niépce creates the first photograph.
- **1839** — Louis Daguerre invents the daguerreotype camera.
- **1840** — Charles Chevalier designs a portrait lens.
- **1841** — William Henry Fox Talbot discovers a way to make prints.
- **1889** — Kodak invents celluloid film.

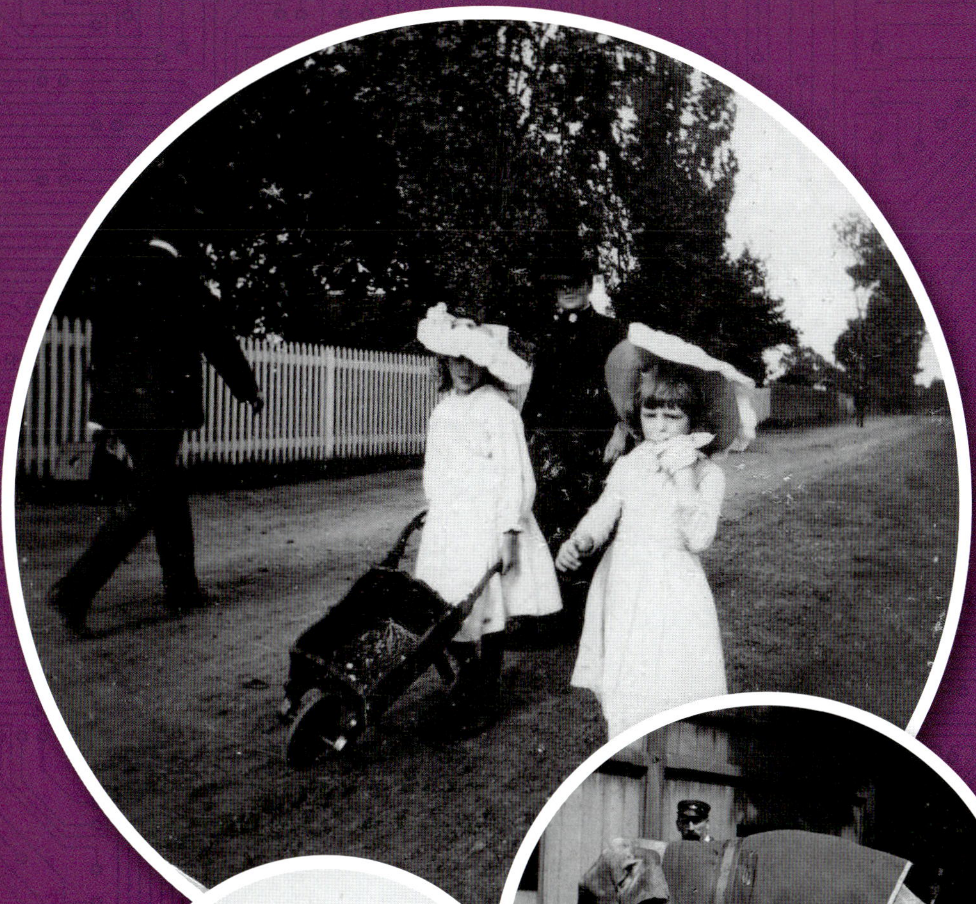

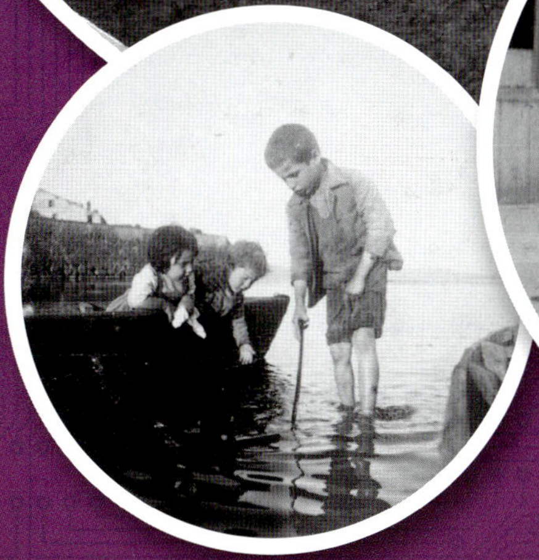

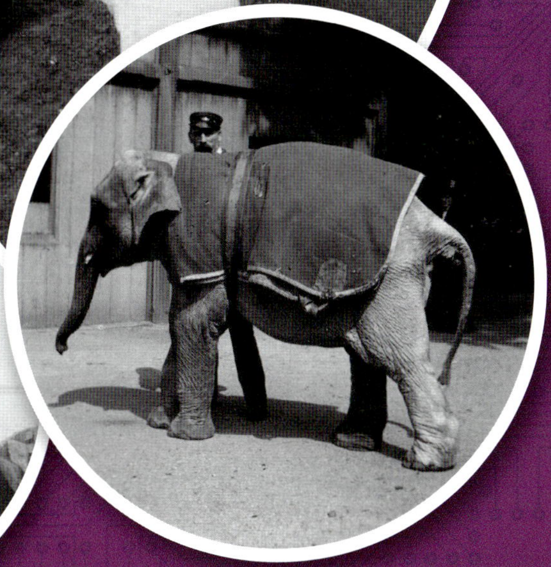

OADING . . . LOADING . . . LOADING . . .

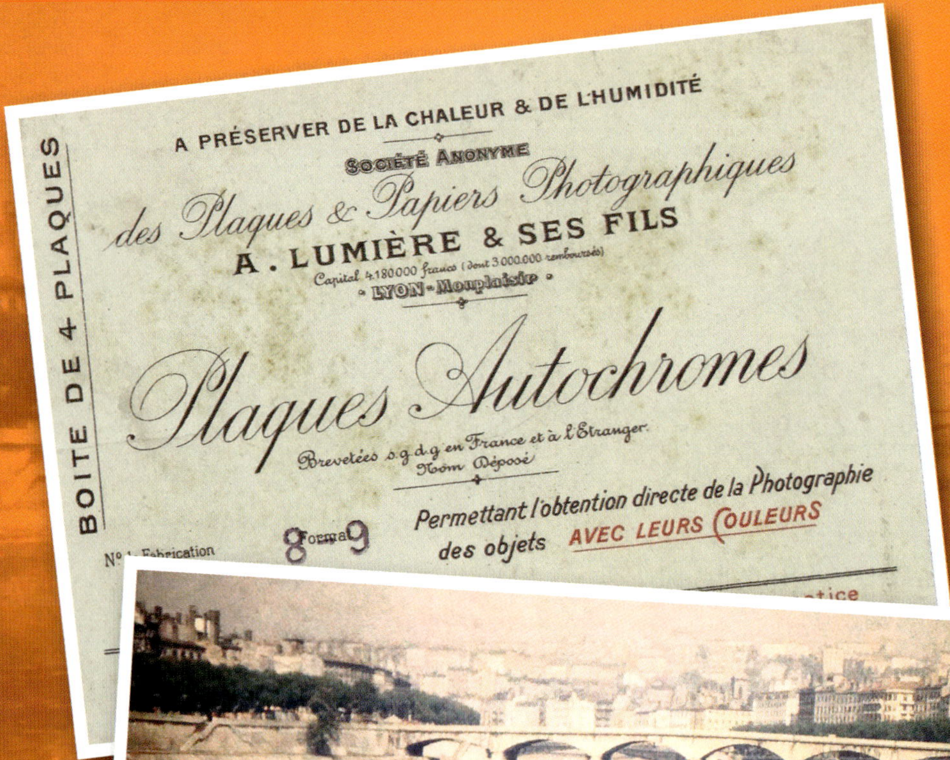

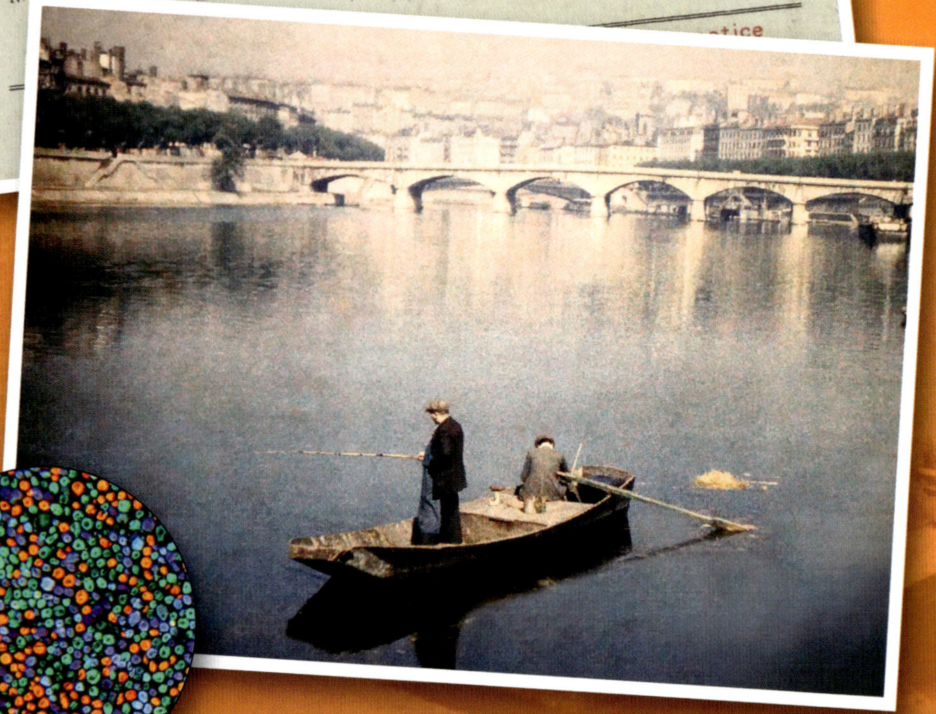

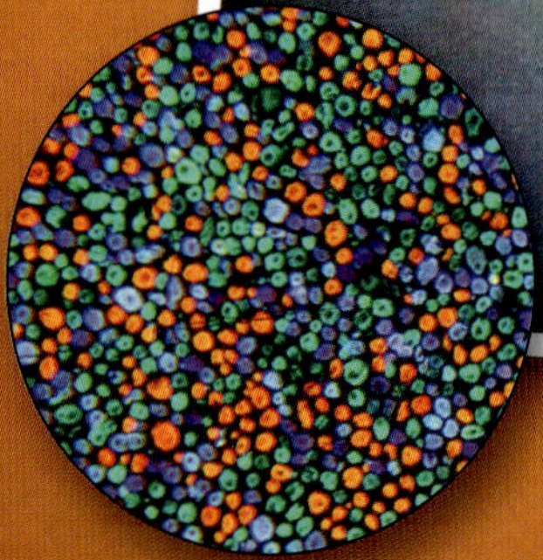

Artists use pinhole cameras to create pictures.	Nicéphore Niépce creates the first photograph.	Louis Daguerre invents the daguerreotype camera.	Charles Chevalier designs a portrait lens.	William Henry Fox Talbot discovers a way to make prints.	Kodak invents celluloid film.
1500s	1827	1839	1840	1841	1889

Since photography began, people had tried to make color photos. Attempts were costly or difficult. In 1907, Auguste and Louis Lumiére showed autochrome color to the public. They dyed tiny grains orange, green, and violet. Then, they painted the grains on a negative. The grains brought out the colors in pictures.

The Lumiéres sold packages of plates (top) with the colored grains (inset) to take autochromes like this one of Lyon, France.

1907 LOADING . . . LOADING . . .

The Lumiere brothers debut autochrome color photography.

Modern Cameras

Today, cameras can be smaller than a juice box. Early cameras were large. The negatives had to be as large as the printed pictures. In 1913, Oskar Barnack designed a handheld camera. It used 35mm film. This narrow film was invented in 1891 for movie cameras. People could make prints bigger when they were developed.

Cameras that used 35mm film (foreground) were smaller and easier to handle, thanks to Oskar Barnack (top).

- 1500s: Artists use pinhole cameras to create pictures.
- 1827: Nicéphore Niépce creates the first photograph.
- 1839: Louis Daguerre invents the daguerreotype camera.
- 1840: Charles Chevalier designs a portrait lens.
- 1841: William Henry Fox Talbot discovers a way to make prints.
- 1889: Kodak invents celluloid film.

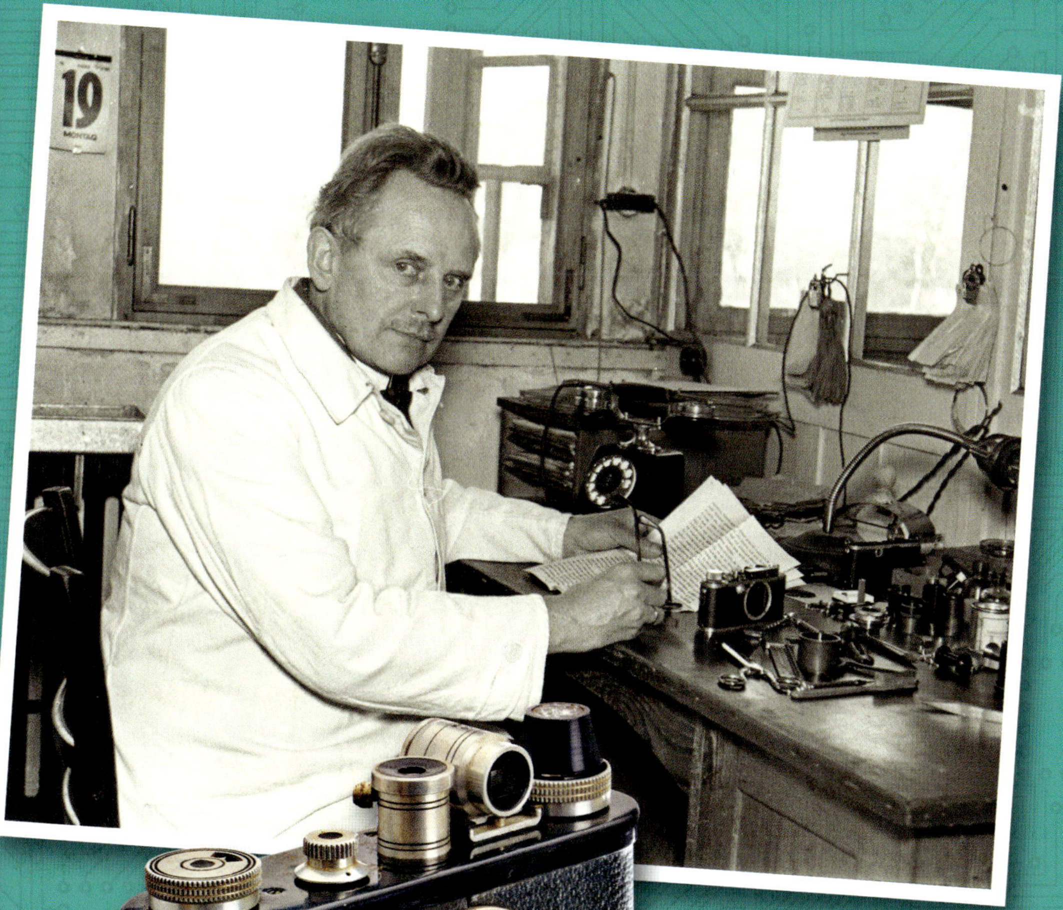

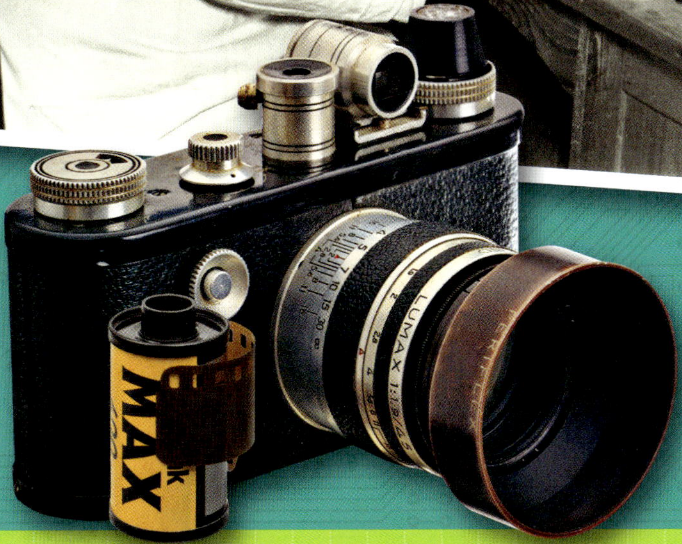

Oscar Barnack designs a 35mm camera.

1907

1913

ING . . . LOADING . . .

The Lumiere brothers debut autochrome color photography.

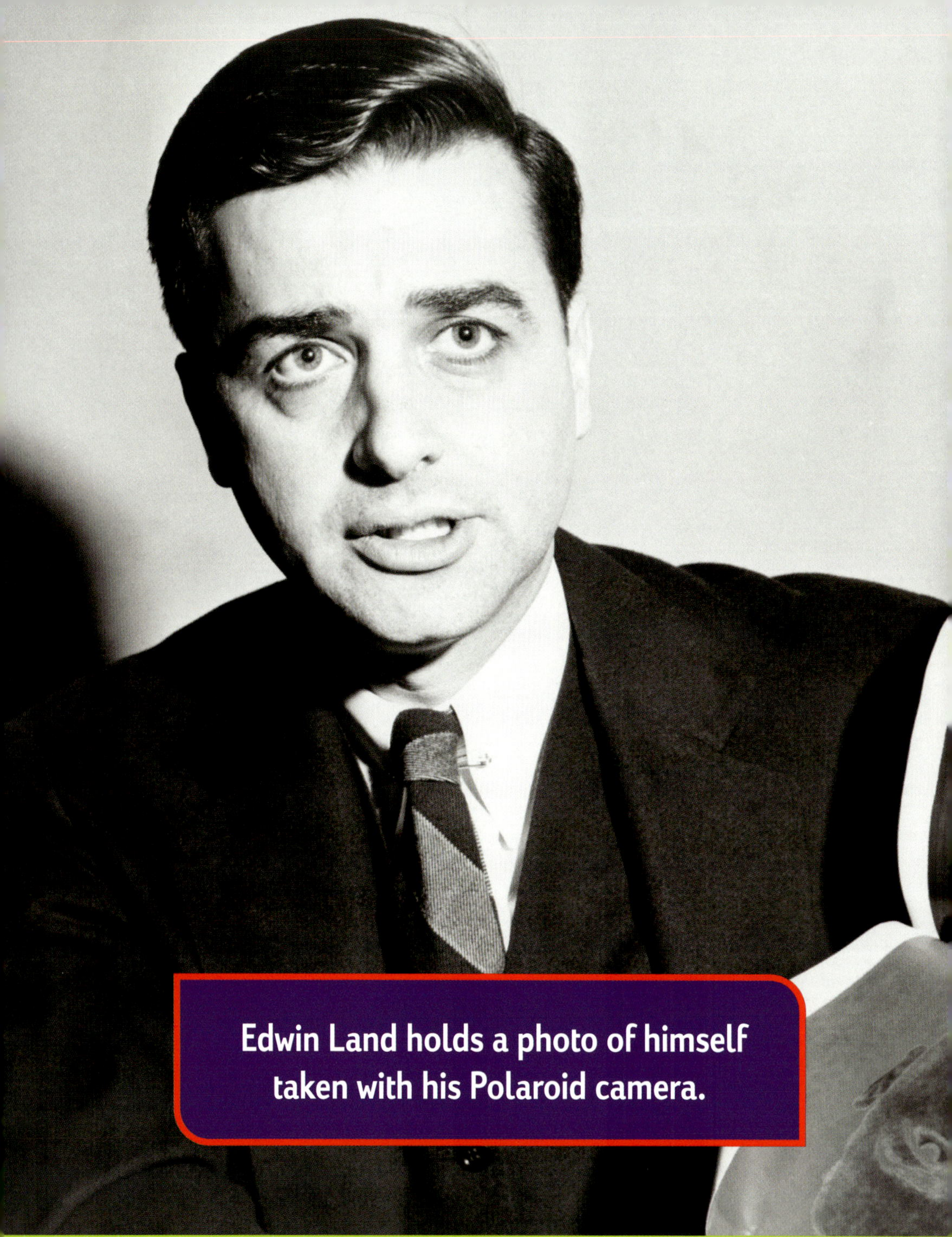

Edwin Land holds a photo of himself taken with his Polaroid camera.

- 1500s: Artists use pinhole cameras to create pictures.
- 1827: Nicéphore Niépce creates the first photograph.
- 1839: Louis Daguerre invents the daguerreotype camera.
- 1840: Charles Chevalier designs a portrait lens.
- 1841: William Henry Fox Talbot discovers a way to make prints.
- 1889: Kodak invents celluloid film.

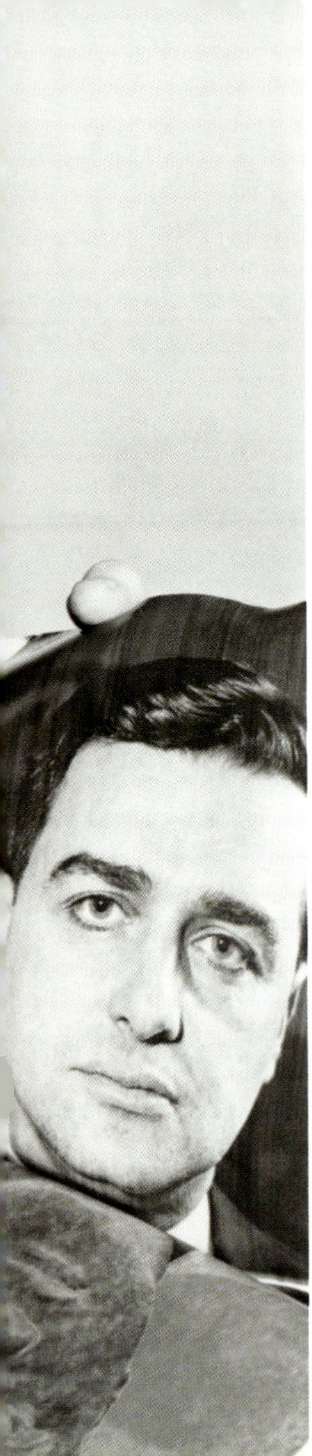

For years, people took film to a store to get prints. They waited days to see their pictures. In 1948, Edwin Land invented the Polaroid camera. Its film held chemicals inside. The picture developed right after it was taken. It was ready within 60 seconds.

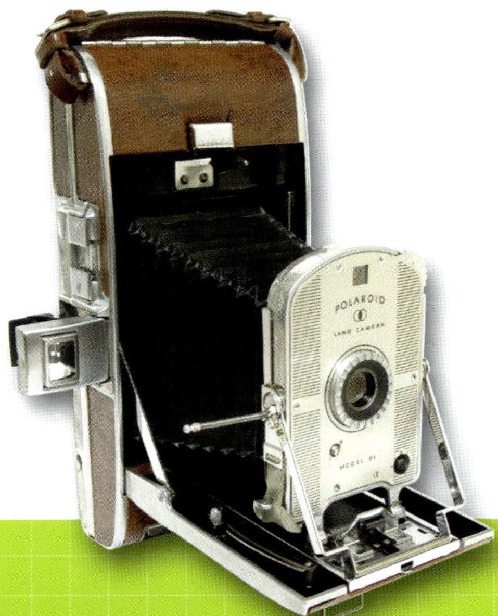

1907 — The Lumiere brothers debut autochrome color photography.

1913 — Oscar Barnack designs a 35mm camera.

1948 — Edwin Land creates instant photos.

...LOADING...

Others made taking pictures easier. In 1977, Konica sold the first point-and-shoot camera. Up until then, people turned the lens by hand to change focus. This camera used an autofocus lens. **Sensors** found the main object in the picture. A motor quickly put the lens at the correct spot.

An ad for the Konica C-35 showed you didn't even have to look at the camera to take a picture.

1500s	Artists use pinhole cameras to create pictures.
1827	Nicéphore Niépce creates the first photograph.
1839	Louis Daguerre invents the daguerreotype camera.
1840	Charles Chevalier designs a portrait lens.
1841	William Henry Fox Talbot discovers a way to make prints.
1889	Kodak invents celluloid film.

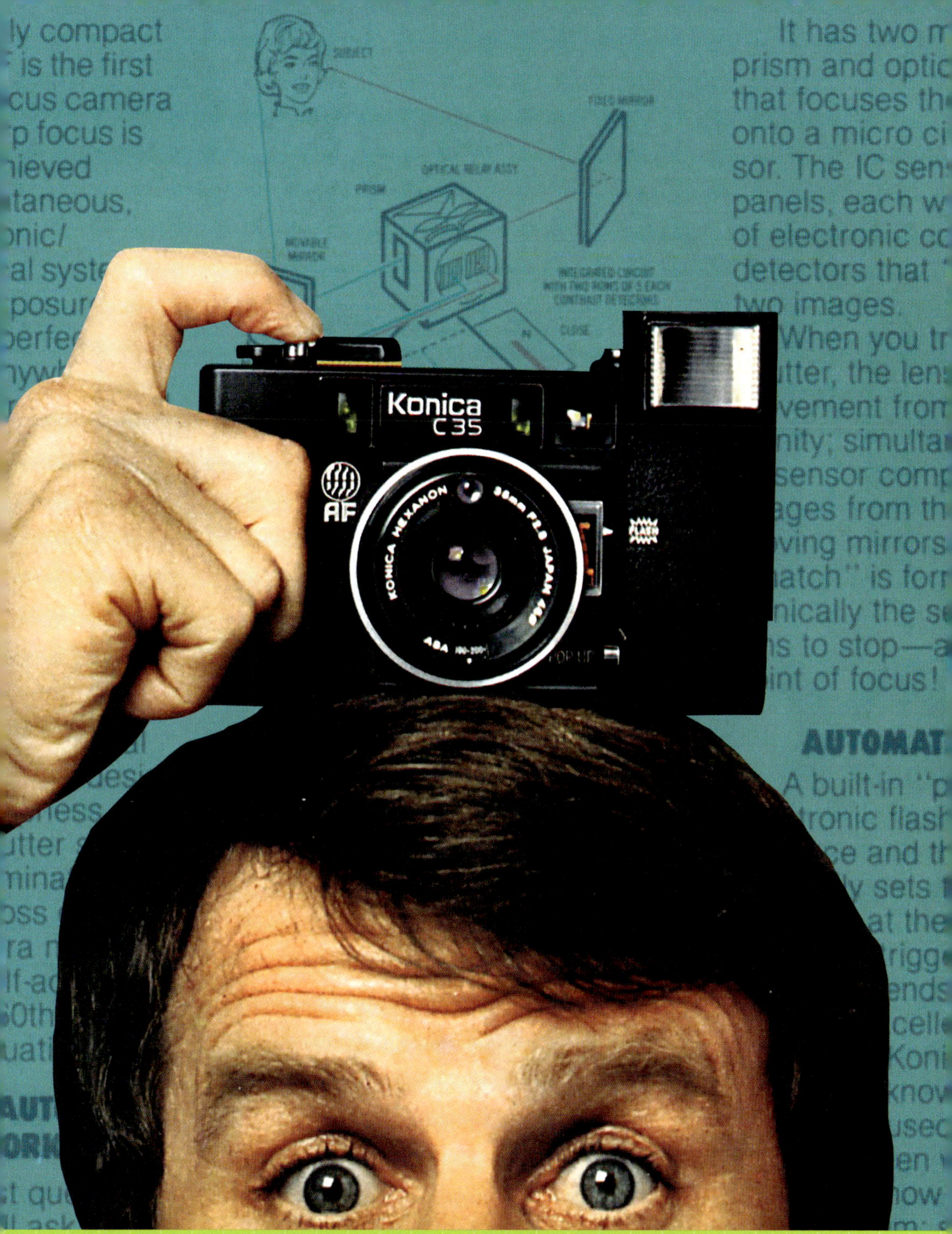

1907	1913	1948	1977
The Lumiere brothers debut autochrome color photography.	Oscar Barnack designs a 35mm camera.	Edwin Land creates instant photos.	Konica sells the first point-and-shoot camera.

ADING . . .

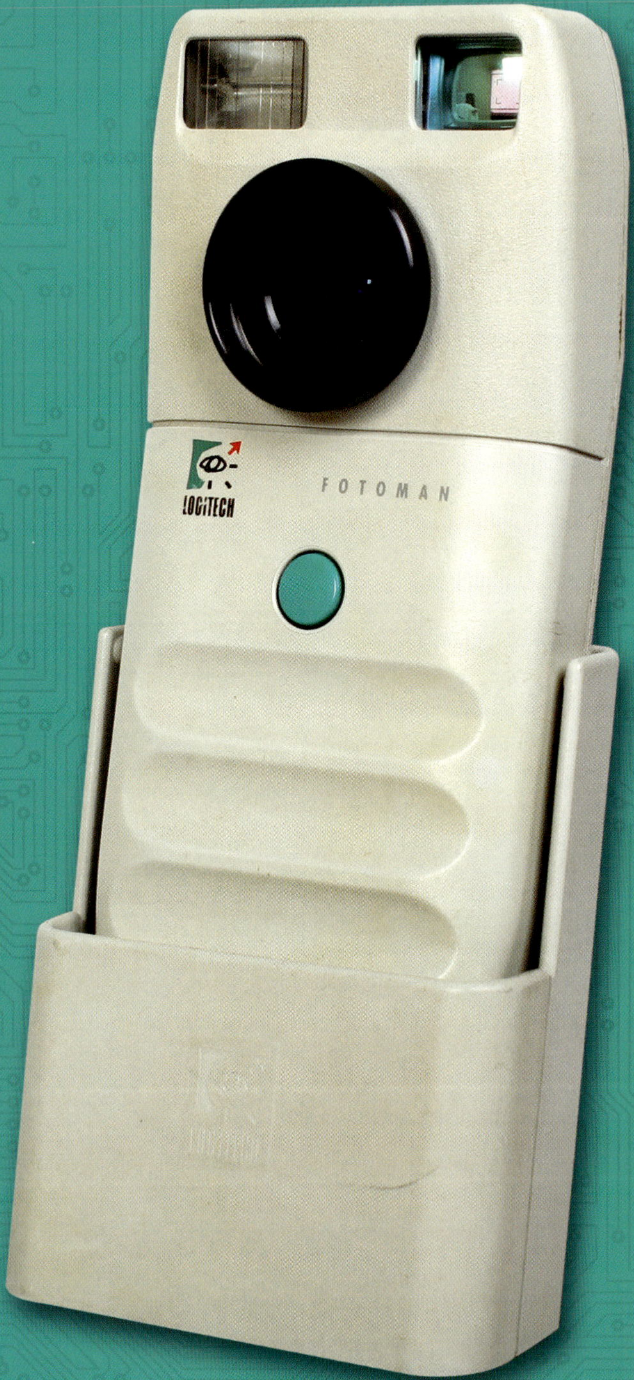

1500s	1827	1839	1840	1841	1889
Artists use pinhole cameras to create pictures.	Nicéphore Niépce creates the first photograph.	Louis Daguerre invents the daguerreotype camera.	Charles Chevalier designs a portrait lens.	William Henry Fox Talbot discovers a way to make prints.	Kodak invents celluloid film.

In 1989, Fuji offered the first digital camera for sale in Japan. Its electronic sensors turned pictures into **pixels**. Each tiny dot held a piece of the picture. The picture was stored electronically. The photos could be sent to a computer. People could look at them before deciding what to print.

The Fotoman was the first digital camera for sale in the United States, in 1993.

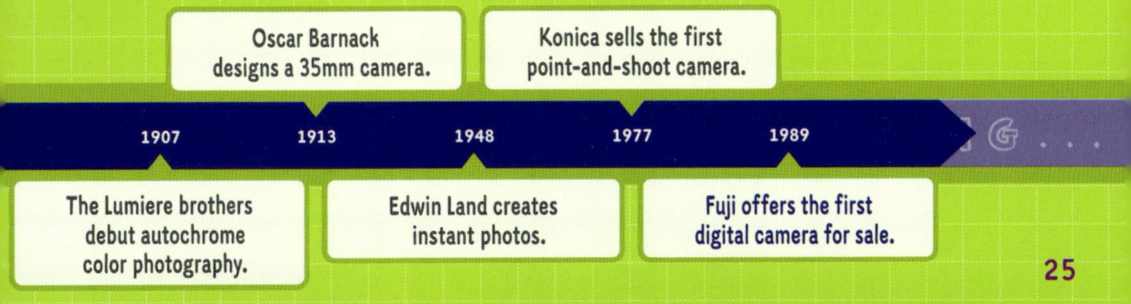

Before long, people didn't need a separate camera. In 2000, Sharp made the first cell phone with a built-in digital camera. Camera phones became the new way to take and send pictures. They led to the rise of picture **apps** like Instagram and Snapchat. Cool editing tools added fun to picture taking.

Early camera phones in North America were flip phones with small screens.

- 1500s: Artists use pinhole cameras to create pictures.
- 1827: Nicéphore Niépce creates the first photograph.
- 1839: Louis Daguerre invents the daguerreotype camera.
- 1840: Charles Chevalier designs a portrait lens.
- 1841: William Henry Fox Talbot discovers a way to make prints.
- 1889: Kodak invents celluloid film.

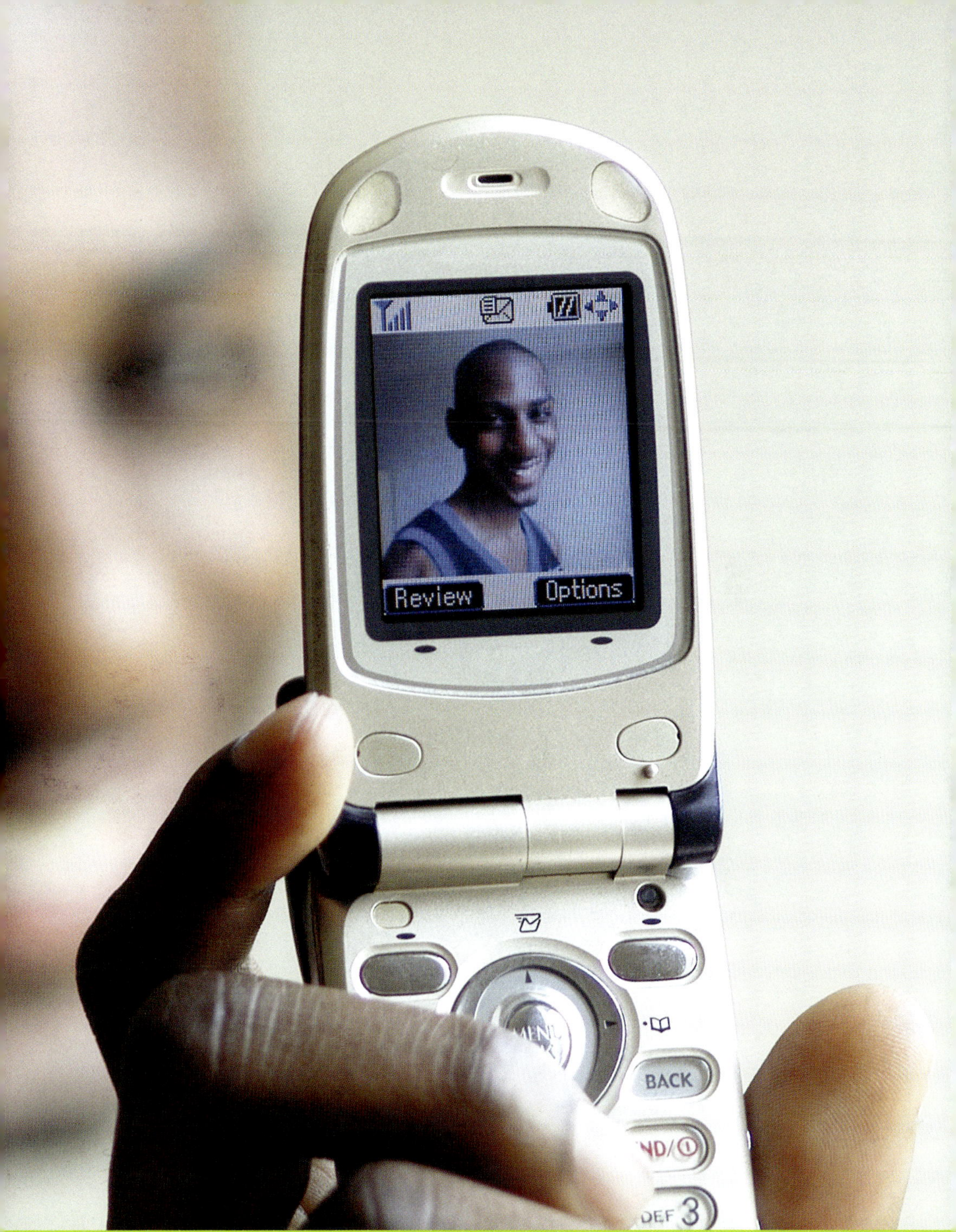

1907	The Lumiere brothers debut autochrome color photography.
1913	Oscar Barnack designs a 35mm camera.
1948	Edwin Land creates instant photos.
1977	Konica sells the first point-and-shoot camera.
1989	Fuji offers the first digital camera for sale.
2000	Sharp sells the first camera phone.

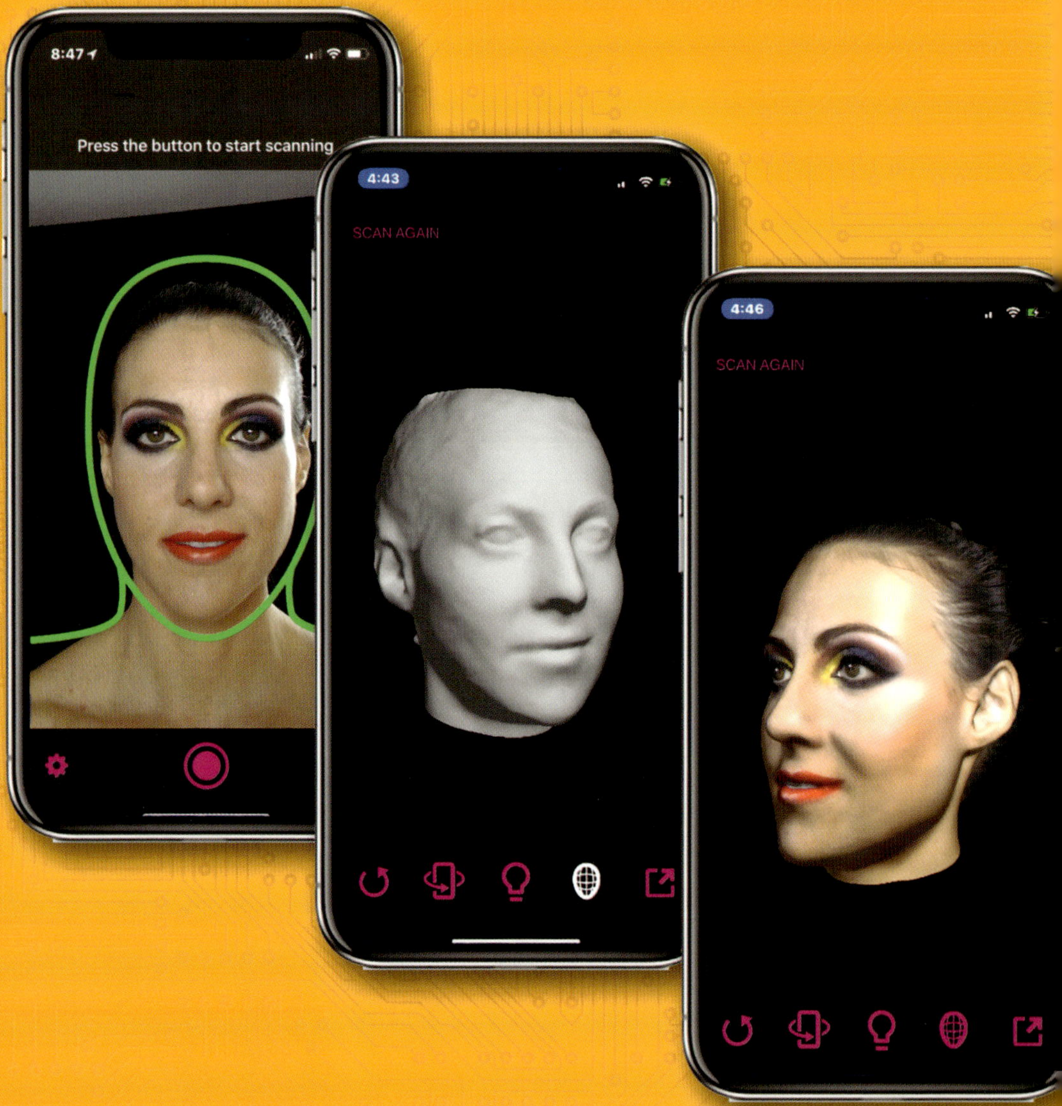

Year	Event
1500s	Artists use pinhole cameras to create pictures.
1827	Nicéphore Niépce creates the first photograph.
1839	Louis Daguerre invents the daguerreotype camera.
1840	Charles Chevalier designs a portrait lens.
1841	William Henry Fox Talbot discovers a way to make prints.
1889	Kodak invents celluloid film.

Into the Future!

Smartphone cameras keep improving. They have stronger sensors and more, larger pixels. Some phones now have two cameras to take **3-D** photos. Photos can even be printed in 3-D. Someday, maybe selfies will pop out of the screen!

A variety of apps let you do a 3-D scan or 3-D photo to share online.

- 1907: The Lumiere brothers debut autochrome color photography.
- 1913: Oscar Barnack designs a 35mm camera.
- 1948: Edwin Land creates instant photos.
- 1977: Konica sells the first point-and-shoot camera.
- 1989: Fuji offers the first digital camera for sale.
- 2000: Sharp sells the first camera phone.

Glossary

app A program used on a computer; "app" stands for application.

bitumen A sticky, black material often made from tar.

celluloid A tough plastic strip of film used to make photographs and movies.

develop To make a picture from film using chemicals.

film A roll of plastic strip used to take photographs.

focus The point at which an image is formed by a lens.

image A picture made by a device.

negative A photograph where the subject's light and dark areas are reversed.

pixel One of the tiny colored dots that form a picture on a computer screen.

plate A flat sheet of glass or metal used to print photographs.

print A physical copy of a picture.

sensor An instrument that picks up changes in light, heat, sound, or movement.

3-D Having a feeling of depth within a flat picture; "3-D" stands for three-dimensional.

Read More

Colby, Jennifer. *Black and White Photographs to Instagram.* Then to Now Tech. Ann Arbor, Mich.: Cherry Lake Publishing, 2019.

Grack, Rachel. *Movies from Then to Now.* Sequence: Developments in Technology. Mankato, Minn.: Amicus /Amicus Ink, 2020.

Stuckey, Rachel. *Get into Photography.* Get into It Guides. St. Catharines, Ontario: Crabtree Publishing Company, 2017.

Websites

National Geographic Kids: Time-Lapse Photography
https://kids.nationalgeographic.com/videos/spectacular-science/#/343044163825

Smithsonian: History of Color Photography
www.smithsonianmag.com/videos/category/smithsonian-channel/the-history-of-color-photography

Ted Ed: From Camera Obscura to Camera Phone
https://ed.ted.com/lessons/illuminating-photography-eva-timothy

Index

About the Author

Rachel Grack has worked in children's nonfiction publishing since 1999. Rachel lives on a small desert ranch in Arizona. She enjoys spending time with her family and barnyard of animals. Thanks to our wireless world, her ranch stays tapped into developing technology.